THE GRIEF JOURNEY

HOPE AND HELP FOR NAVIGATING LOSS

Foreword by Rob Parsons, OBE

With thanks to Lisa Higgins, Sammi Bryan, Esther Holt, Jess Hills, Paula Pridham, and the Specialist Support Team at Care for the Family. Special thanks to Yvonne Tulloch (CEO, AtaLoss) and Wendy Jones (Specialist Support Advisor, Care for the Family) for their contributions and expertise.

A CIP catalogue record for this book is available from the British Library.
ISBN: 978-1-7397407-5-7

Cover design and illustration by Beth Stevenson, Care for the Family.
Typeset by John Lambert, breathe.design
Printed and bound by Xpedient Print Services.

A Christian initiative to strengthen family life, offering support to everyone.
Care for the Family is a registered charity (England and Wales: 1066905; Scotland: SC038497). A company limited by guarantee no. 3482910.
Registered in England and Wales. Tovey House, Cleppa Park, Newport, NP10 8BA.

CONTENTS

FOREWORD

'Loss is part of life. Sorrow is part of living and loving. Grief is part of the journey.'[1]

– Malcolm Duncan

'I'm sorry to tell you that Ronnie has had another stroke, Mr Parsons. You might want to come and see him as soon as you can.'

I ended the call, replaying the nurse's words in my heart, and my wife Dianne and I drove straight to the hospital. We held his hand as he died and told him we loved him. Ronnie, a dear friend who had been part of our family for longer than our own children, had left us.

Whenever Dianne and I have had to walk that road of grief, we have been blessed not to travel it alone. Friends and family were there for us at Ronnie's death, as well as in other losses, and while it does not take the pain away, it reassures us that we are not alone. A companion through grief really does make a difference.

I've noticed this time and again at our bereavement support weekends for parents who have lost a child, siblings who have lost their brother or sister, and

---

[1] Malcolm Duncan, *Good Grief* (Monarch, 2020) p.19.

those widowed young. From the start, the people who run these events have always been those who have experienced a similar loss. This helps them offer those grieving a sense that others have trod this path before – there are those who understand what it's like, who are with you in this.

In supporting bereaved people we've always found that the most important thing is not to have clever answers, but to give a sense of identification and understanding; and to listen. This is what we aim to offer you in this little book.

People will sometimes say to us as we grieve, 'Time will heal' but of course it doesn't; how can it? But as the years go by it may be possible for us to find what many call 'a new normal'. Grief changes us – none of us escape unscathed – but you can find your way towards hope again. We pray this book will be a trusted companion to help you along the way.

Rob Parsons, OBE
Founder and Chairman, Care for the Family

INTRODUCTION

We will all experience bereavement at some point in our lives, but that does not mean it is easy to face. In the West, we don't seem to be comfortable talking about death, and so we can be left feeling ill-prepared when someone close to us dies.

You may have picked up this book looking for some explanation of the complex emotions you're feeling, or for practical ideas and support. Having experienced loss ourselves, our aim in this book is to give you these things and more, but we also hope you get a sense that you are not alone. And that, although life won't ever be the same because of the huge gap left by your bereavement, there is a life still to be lived, and there can be light in the future ahead. More than anything else, in our most difficult moments we all need a sense of hope.

Please feel free to dip in and out of this book, and don't feel that you have to read it all at once. It may be that some sections are more helpful for you than others at different points in your journey through grief. We have also included quotes from a range of people talking about their loss. While your experience may be different, as each journey is unique, we hope that some of them will resonate and be helpful.

CHAPTER ONE
FIRST IMPACT

'Getting through a bereavement is like riding a bucking bronco. The saddle is no place to sit quietly and contemplate ... it's all we can do to keep our fingers gripped to its mane. And just hope we don't fall off.'[2]

– Virginia Ironside

When someone significant to us dies, the impact on us can be huge. Many people experience a profound sense of shock – even if this loss was expected. This shock can affect us physically and emotionally. Sometimes people feel numb, as if they are functioning on 'autopilot'. Insomnia, loss of appetite, chest tightness, difficulty

[2] Virginia Ironside, *'You'll Get Over It': The Rage of Bereavement* (Penguin, 1997), p.61.

breathing or swallowing, or feeling cold, are also common responses. We might feel detached from our emotions, and be unable to express how we feel, or be completely overwhelmed with emotion. These are all normal reactions. Whether you are angry, sad, relieved, exhausted, numb or a mixture of all of these, know that you're not alone in feeling this way.

IT'S NORMAL TO FEEL COMPLETELY OVERWHELMED

There are so many different emotions that we might experience (see Chapter 2 for more on this). If our loved one was ill for a long time, we may feel relieved that they are no longer suffering – although this can be accompanied by feelings of guilt. We might feel a deep sense of bewilderment and frustration if the death was sudden and/or due to complicated circumstances. Whatever age they were when they died, and however it happened, it will probably feel unfair as we have been robbed of the years that we could otherwise have had with them. We can feel a deep disconnect with the outside world, especially as life around us goes on as normal when it feels inconceivable to us that it ever could, or should, again. We might also experience a sense of denial – that the death doesn't feel real and we can't believe it has happened.

If we had a difficult relationship with the person who has died, or had become estranged from them, we might have particularly mixed emotions. It's common to feel angry too, with doctors, ourselves or maybe with God – whether or not we believe in him.

Practicalities can feel overwhelming. Simple tasks we used to undertake easily can be suddenly beyond us. 'Brain fog' can make it feel as if we can no longer cope with even the smallest things and we may feel exhausted all of the time. Breaking the news to others might feel especially difficult. If possible, enlist the help of others to do so, particularly if it will involve making a lot of phone calls or responding to comments on a social media announcement. This can be the case with funeral arrangements too, so do try to get support with this (see page 14 for more advice on this).

However you feel, you are not the only one. You're not going crazy, and you won't feel like this for ever.

> 'When we first lose someone, it can be like [a canyon] emotionally and physically. There is this gaping, dangerous hole that you absolutely know is there, but it's fogged over because of the emotional pain, and with the knowledge that what we can see is not quite the full picture. We can't quite comprehend all that has happened.' – RUTH

ROUTINES AND RITUALS

While we may want to hide away and not speak to anyone, it is often helpful to keep to a routine (whether old or new). Bereavement is a time of significant change, and routines ground us and ensure that we take care of ourselves (for example through eating three meals a day, or going for a daily walk – see Chapter 3 for more on this). It is best to avoid impulsive decisions and excessive busyness – while they may seem like helpful distractions, they can stop us from being able to process our grief.

It can be hard to deal with the expectation to 'get over' our loss that we may feel from others. 'Getting over' loss can be an unhelpful concept: most people find it more helpful to think of life after bereavement as an ongoing adjustment, as we learn to grow around our grief (see page 40). This reflects the fact that life is not the same as before and it will take time to get used to. There may be a yearning for life to get back to normal, but there is no need to rush the process of grief.

It can be hard to find the right rituals to help us navigate our mourning, especially as our modern culture has done away with so many of them. In centuries past, families used to dress in mourning clothes for a significant period, in order to signify their loss to others. There was an expectation that grief would take time, and society as a whole accepted and acknowledged this. Today, death is usually a taboo topic of conversation, which means we can feel ill-prepared. And those around us who have not experienced bereavement may be deeply uncomfortable talking about it, which means we may have less support than we truly need.

'Those first days after my husband died did not feel real. It was as if I was watching myself from a distance while on autopilot. There were so many people showing up at the house, but I just wanted them to go away. I knew they meant well, but I needed space. Decisions had to be made regarding the funeral and, due to the nature of his death, there was an investigation. While our Family Liaison Officer was lovely, I was being asked questions that I was just not able to process due to the trauma I was experiencing.

Attending the funeral was an emotionally heightened experience. There are parts of the day that I just don't remember, while other parts I remember vividly. I know that I spoke to so many people, but I can only recall some of these conversations. I went from moments of intense weeping to moments of stunned silence. What I vividly recall was the looks on the faces of my three children. The intense pain on their tiny faces created a resolve that I would walk this journey, and I would walk it as well as I possibly could.' – DANIELLE

ATTENDING THE FUNERAL

Before the funeral, it may be possible to see the body of your loved one if you wish to. You may come from a culture or tradition where it is normal for family members to wash and dress their body, or even keep them in your own home for a few days before burial. Even if this is not the case, you might feel that seeing the body will help you accept the reality of what has happened. Others will prefer to remember the person as they were when they were alive. Whatever your preference, try not to be swayed by others' opinions and instead do what you feel is best for you.

Many people find that the funeral (or a thanksgiving service) is a helpful part of 'saying goodbye', to a loved one, but it can feel quite daunting too. While it may be comforting to have the support of others around us, sometimes people can say unhelpful things (see Chapter 6), or it can feel like we're having to comfort them instead of the other way around. Maybe there are estranged family members who will be present, or other family tensions complicating the day. Depending on those around us, we might feel under pressure to 'keep a stiff upper lip', or to be more demonstrative and to show visible grief. Try not to let the weight of other people's expectations overwhelm you: this is a time to focus on what works for *you*.

AFTER THE FUNERAL

The days and weeks immediately after a funeral can be very hard, as this is generally when the reality of life without our loved one begins to sink in. Some of us may crave some space to process our emotions, but may now be caring for children on our own or supporting an elderly relative, and so have little time to ourselves. For others of us, it is the silence that is most difficult to deal with, especially if we are now living alone. Utilising background noise such as a radio or smartphone can be helpful through the day and also at night-time.

If we have lost our spouse or partner, with whom we did all the mundane, everyday things and who was with us through all the good and bad experiences of life, we can feel overwhelmed by loneliness as well as grief. The house suddenly feels so empty, and there are reminders of our loved one everywhere, which can be very difficult to deal with.

Some of us will long for company, but find that all the offers of help drop off after a while and no one will look directly at us as they aren't sure what to say. Whatever your experience, be gentle on yourself as you adjust to life without your loved one.

REMEMBER

- The impact of bereavement can be huge – it is totally normal to experience a whole range of emotions and physical effects.
- Take time to look after yourself and find routines that work for you.
- Do not allow others' expectations to influence you.

CHAPTER TWO

THE ROLLERCOASTER OF GRIEF

'When Jim died, I found myself in the centre of an emotional storm. I could no more control my feelings than I could stop the trees in the garden tossing around in a gale. The feelings went everywhere: anger, guilt, despair, loneliness, doubt, anxiety, all tossing about in my head like a cage of angry monkeys.'[3]

– Philippa Skinner

Grieving can feel like being trapped on a rollercoaster, with no means of getting off. Sometimes we may feel that we're on a smooth section of track, with emotions on an even keel. But then a sudden drop or turn can

[3] Philippa Skinner, *See You Soon: A mother's story of drugs, grief and hope* (Presence Books, 2012), p.110.

make it seem as though the ground has dropped out from beneath us. We cannot emphasise enough that this is *normal*.

Grief affects us psychologically in a number of ways, emotionally, physically, cognitively and behaviourally. Knowing what might happen can help us feel less alone when we feel like we are being pummelled by extreme reactions we have no control over.

EMOTIONAL

We will each have our own ideas about how we should deal with grief and how long the grieving process should last for. But grief affects each of us differently and often our own reactions will surprise us.

Guilt is a common reaction to grief. It can hit us if we feel emotionally numb initially and are unable to cry. We think we should be able to show our sadness through tears and feel frustrated and guilty that we can't. We may experience a sense of relief if our loved one had been suffering, but that can lead on to feelings of guilt because we don't think we should be allowed to be relieved. We can begin to question ourselves, causing more guilt: should we have spent more time with them in their final months and days? In cases of suicide or other sudden deaths, we may obsess over whether we could have done something to prevent it and become increasingly frustrated and angry – at ourselves and others.

> 'My mum was ill for many years, and in her last few years took a huge downward turn. Watching her deteriorate physically was incredibly difficult, and when she was no longer able to engage with the things we used to enjoy most together, I realised that I had started grieving well before she died. When she did die it felt partly a relief, that she was no longer in pain, but then such a tide of sadness and guilt hit. Soon after I became numb, watching and supporting my sister and dad as they grieved and feeling like I had no emotions at all, which is very unlike me. It took many months for the tears to begin to flow.'
>
> – CLAIRE

Whatever the cause of death, we may feel angry with them for 'leaving' us. This is completely normal and it is important not to suppress or deny our anger. In time it usually gives way to understanding and compassion for them. There can be a sense of despair over all the opportunities that will now be missed or having to face life without them. It is common to become frustrated and angry about being 'left behind'.

Your mood might swing from day to day and even minute to minute, ranging from an acceptance of the death to deep longing for the loved one's return. Anxiety, panic attacks or fear for surviving loved ones or our own mortality are also common. As time goes on, it may be that tears are triggered for no apparent reason, and a sense of sadness and loss overwhelms us.

COGNITIVE

Grief also impacts the way we think. We may feel as if we are experiencing 'brain fog', and struggle to pay attention to things going on around us. Our minds are so full of the pain, the demands upon us, and just existing that there is no room for anything else. The world can feel like a blur and the things going on around us do not register.

Because we are struggling to pay attention, our memory becomes less effective. In early grief it is likely that we will experience a bombardment of memories of our loved one. There is no room for new memories. Retaining simple bits of information can be a real struggle. It may be that even finding the right word is an almost impossible task. But over time we will become sharper. Our memories will come into focus again.

Decision-making may be necessary following the loss of a loved one, but it is rarely wise to make life-changing decisions at this time. Yet even at an everyday level, where once we were able to act decisively, even simple choices can sometimes become overwhelming. The idea of planning anything, even a shopping trip, is impossible. Choosing tea or coffee may even be a step too far.

An unexpected consequence of grief can be its effects on our vision, and we may find our depth perception becoming diminished. We may feel stupid and clumsy, but we don't need to beat ourselves up about this – it is caused by our grief.

PHYSICAL

While this area is often overlooked, grief can also affect us physically. Many will have difficulty sleeping due to the emotional strain, which can make even the simplest of everyday tasks harder as we are so exhausted. This does usually improve with time and rest, but be aware that insomnia can hit again when something (an anniversary or even an unrelated event) triggers the grief afresh. Or you may find you are sleeping more than normal, and dread waking up and having to face the reality of your loss again. Other physical symptoms that can be caused by grief include:

- chest tightness
- changes in appetite
- sensitivity to noise
- aches and pains
- difficulty breathing

- lack of energy
- dry mouth
- hyperhidrosis (excessive sweating)
- gut/stomach problems

> 'I can still remember the restlessness and exhaustion from lack of sleep. We had been on standby every night for the last ten days of Mum's life, in case hospice nurses weren't available to sit with her. We'd stay up late, snatch a few hours of fitful sleep then be up again early to take over from the night nurse. On the morning Mum died we had been up all night, sitting next to her as it was clear the end was near. It wasn't until 5am that she drew her last breath. For days, weeks and even months after, we all found it hard to sleep. And in the first few weeks myself, my sister and my dad kept finding ourselves waking up at exactly 5am – somehow our brains and bodies were wired with that information and even though we could barely function, we were forced awake. We still find that on her birthday and the date she died we wake up at 5am, and periods of extreme stress can trigger the insomnia again.' – CLAIRE

Be kind to yourself if you find you're not able to cope as well as usual. Keep an eye on any physical symptoms experienced – if they persist or are severe, do get in contact with your doctor. Don't be afraid to accept any offers of help from family and friends – if that gives you a chance to rest, it could be just what you need.

BEHAVIOURAL

We may find that our behaviour changes when we're grieving, in ways that can be quite unexpected. For example, we can become irrational and may act in ways that are out of character. As we struggle with a torrent of emotions – or a lack of them – it can cause us to shut down and be unresponsive, become overly eager to keep ourselves busy or inexplicably irritated by those around us.

We may experience flashbacks or nightmares, have hallucinations of our loved one or become convinced that we've seen them in a crowd, for example. We may have periods of restlessness or hyperactivity or obsess about minor details. This is usually a coping mechanism to distract us from our feelings of grief. On the other hand, we may struggle with basic tasks, 'blanking out' with everyday jobs such as filling the car with petrol or using the right detergent in the dishwasher. Even simple activities like getting out of bed, making meals or showering can be hard work, particularly in the early days of bereavement. We may feel a lack of motivation to face the world each morning, and struggle to cope with all the practicalities that need attending to, such as organising the funeral. This can then generate feelings of guilt, which perpetuates that emotion.

WHEN FEELINGS ARE COMPLICATED

It can be hard if we have mixed feelings about the person we have lost. Perhaps we are grieving for an ex-partner, an estranged friend, or a parent who let us down. It is possible to love a person while recognising that they have at times been damaging to us. Death can be a reprieve from this pain. It is a relief as well as a loss.

The conflicting feelings can elicit guilt. We can feel for example that we 'should' love our parents and grieve their loss. But if the parenting was critical or neglectful, then death may break the power of those negative memories and experiences. Expression of this relief may receive disapproval from people around us as it doesn't fit in with social norms. Navigating these conflicts and coming to terms with your own feelings can be emotionally exhausting.

Being true to yourself and allowing these difficult emotions out will enable better management of your grief. If it is not possible to safely express them, and there is no trusted friend willing to walk empathically through these complicated emotions, journalling can offer a positive outlet.

IT IS ALL NORMAL

These responses may seem extreme or irrational, but in fact they are normal for someone struggling to make sense of the enormous change that a bereavement can bring. And, as we've seen, each part of us affects the other so our emotional, physical, cognitive and behavioural responses are all interlinked. That is why it is so important to look after yourself (see Chapter 3).

REMEMBER

- It is common to experience a whole range of emotions over a long period of time.
- Our physical health is affected by grief, so keep an eye on any symptoms you experience and don't be afraid to get in touch with your doctor.
- Grief can cause us to behave in unexpected ways.

CHAPTER THREE

TAKING CARE OF YOURSELF

'I've never been very good at setting boundaries in my life, but I tried very hard to make sure I set them surrounding my grief. To let myself do whatever I needed to process the loss of my parents and not to let anyone tell me I should be acting or feeling a certain way.'[4]

– Noelle Bailey

Grief can be exhausting mentally, physically and emotionally, and yet we can feel that prioritising our own wellbeing after loss is somehow wrong. We may feel that there is too much to do, so we just don't have time to slow down and consider ourselves. We may even believe that by experiencing loss of appetite or sleep, for

[4] Noelle Bailey, 'Learning from Grief', *griefstories.org*, 7 December 2022.

example, we are honouring our loved one by showing how much we are missing them. However, it is possible to grieve well and look after ourselves at the same time.

LOOKING OUT FOR WARNING SIGNS

When we are in the midst of grief, it can be hard to notice when we are beginning to neglect our own wellbeing, so here are some signs that might indicate a need to prioritise self-care:

Unusual sleeping patterns.
Sleep is often one of the main things affected by grief. When trying to sleep, your mind may race or it might be hard to stay asleep for long. Allowing ourselves to nap when we feel tired is helpful in the first days after bereavement. If you are experiencing insomnia or excessive fatigue it would be best to visit your doctor for advice.

Alcohol or drug dependence.
Reaching for a glass of wine, cigarette or other drug (including painkillers or prescription drugs) in order to unwind may seem like a harmless thing to do. However, becoming dependent on an outside substance in order to cope will not be helpful in the long term. For example, it is important to remember that alcohol acts as a depressant in the body, intensifying negative emotions such as shame or sadness. While it may feel like it is bringing short-term relief, it can have an adverse effect on our mood and impair everyday activities.

Binge eating or ongoing appetite loss.

It can seem like too much effort to cook a healthy meal while we are grieving. Some of us may binge on our favourite high-fat or high-sugar foods instead, looking to them for comfort, or we may find that we have lost our appetite completely. Some of this may be inevitable in the short term – perhaps we're fuelling ourselves on coffee and doughnuts between stints at a dying relative's side, or we simply can't bring ourselves to eat more than a few mouthfuls at a time following our loved one's death. But if this becomes a longer-lasting pattern, it can potentially be harmful to our health, and keep us from processing our emotions. As far as is possible, try to keep to a regular meal schedule and choose healthy foods where you can.

Distraction and suppression.

We all experience and cope with grief in our own individual ways, but processing our emotions rather than avoiding them is an important step in the grief journey. So if we recognise that, rather than simply taking a break for a short while, we are intentionally distracting ourselves or suppressing our emotions in an ongoing way so that we don't have to deal with them, it may be time to gently begin to allow them to surface so we can process them.

Avoiding social situations.

It is normal in the early days to try to avoid situations where we might have to explain our loss. We may also find we don't want to go to places we normally like because of the emotional cost of putting on a brave face in public. There isn't a set time when it's advisable to start facing these situations again. However, if you find yourself no longer able to face any social situation, or you are avoiding places you really need to go, then it's a good idea to look for help. Maybe a friend could go with you, or check on you part-way through an occasion.

Reassurance seeking.
After loss it is normal to feel anxious about making decisions, or feel a need for reassurance from others when we do. Sometimes though it can reach a point where we feel paralysed, unable to function or make any decisions. If this is what you are experiencing, asking a friend to support you as you try to start making decisions again would be helpful.

BEING GENTLE ON YOURSELF

Do remember that the early days of grief can be exhausting and that can reduce our overall capacity to cope with life. There is nothing wrong in cutting back on commitments, or in taking up offers for help (or directly asking others for it) so that we don't have as much to deal with. Recognise that stressful situations may cause extreme responses in this time of heightened emotion, and make allowances for yourself (and others) if this happens.

Some of us will find crying difficult, while for others it seems almost impossible to stop the tears. Sometimes we need to deliberately give ourselves time and space to cry. It's good to be aware that crying is only one form of expressing grief. As long as you are processing the grief, it's OK. Some people may find that they don't cry and find it easier to process their grief in different ways (for example through talking, or taking long walks). It can also be really helpful to write down thoughts and feelings in a journal in order to make sense of what has happened.

Reaching out to a non-judgemental friend in order to talk things through can also be helpful, although, for some, this can feel too difficult to begin with, and that's OK as long as you don't completely isolate yourself. In the early days of bereavement it may be easier, in fact, to speak to someone outside the situation who can offer a listening ear, such as a hospice chaplain (who can be a safe person to talk to, whether or not you have a faith). Do remember that close friends, although they might not always get things right, will want to be there for you too. Be open to those you trust checking in on you – it might not be comfortable at the time, but it is a helpful means of support.

> 'Rev Steven was the chaplain at the hospice who provided end-of-life care for my wife Sue, and he visited us weekly as Sue's health deteriorated. Following Sue's death, Steven rang me and asked if I would like him to visit me. As an atheist I was not sure if this would help. However, as I had found his previous visits helpful, I agreed. We met several times and I discovered he was the only non-family person I was able to open my heart to, as I found it extremely difficult to discuss things with friends. To be able to discuss your feelings about how you will cope with the future, without having to worry about how this will impact on your family, was in a way liberating. I found Steven's support invaluable as he had a wealth of experience in dealing with bereavement. He became a crucial part of the jigsaw when coping with all the emotions and practicalities.' – RANDALL

INTENTIONAL SELF-CARE

Having a daily routine is important, particularly on those days when we just want to hide under the duvet all day. Taking a shower or having a bath daily will help, as will getting out into the fresh air every day. Even a short walk round the block is a good start. Remember that exercise releases endorphins, which lift our mood.

While grief can feel all-consuming, we do need to take a break from the intensity of the emotions from time to time. It may feel like you can't enjoy anything at all right now, but try to make the effort to engage with hobbies or other activities that you usually enjoy. If you find you do end up enjoying them, don't feel bad for doing so.

We need to allow ourselves time and space to grieve, but there will inevitably be situations that we have to face. Working out ways to cope with anything that might be difficult beforehand can remove the extra level of stress.

> 'In work situations, I found having "an escape route" a very useful tool for coping. For example, I was due to play the piano for the school Christmas concert only four months after losing my son. I chose to record all the music beforehand and had someone ready just to press "play" if I needed to get out. Just having that escape route there enabled me to cope and I played for the whole concert. Planning an escape route helped me in many situations over the years and I often didn't use them – they just needed to be there.' – JANE

SEEKING HELP

Our society has begun to recognise the benefits of asking for help and so the phrase 'It's OK not to feel OK' is one that most of us will have heard today. However, we can still struggle to apply this to ourselves. It is important to realise that it is not a sign of weakness to seek help in recovery from the depths of grief. Rather, it is strong to admit when we need others and to accept help in getting better.

It may be wise to seek help if, after a period of months or years, you find that your grief is still intense and overwhelming, or if:

- Your mood is low for a long period
- You are unable to eat, sleep, shower or otherwise take care of yourself well
- You avoid company and neglect hobbies that used to interest you

There are a lot of bereavement support options out there, but it is important to consider which of them may be right for you. Some people will benefit from a greater level of support such as counselling, while others prefer to mostly find support from others who understand their situation, perhaps through groups or befriending (see Useful Resources on page 113 for more details).

Befriending services.

Befriending involves being matched up with someone who has also been through grief (often a similar circumstance), so is more likely to understand. It may be telephone support or in person, but a befriender will always seek to be an empathetic listening ear. There are a range of befriending services available, some specialist and some general (see Useful Resources on page 113 for more details).

Local support groups.

Like befriending, support groups offer peer support from those who have been through bereavement too. The mutual support these groups offer can be a real lifeline. There are specialist groups, such as those helping men overcome grief through retreats together. Others are support weekends for bereaved parents, siblings or spouses. Some might be unstructured, with a focus on time to chat informally. Others might go through helpful material for discussion such as *The Bereavement Journey* (thebereavementjourney.org).

> 'I heard about a forthcoming Widowed Young support weekend in May, and knew I needed to be there. People said to me, "Aren't you brave, to go on your own so soon!" But I wasn't brave at all; I was desperately seeking help. And I did find help. There was something healing about being with others who had walked the same path as me, and understood my feelings.'
>
> – ANNE

Organisations offering these groups may be a national or local bereavement charity, a local faith centre or other community group.

Online support.
Telephone or live chat services can be good options for a one-off chat at a particularly low moment. They can also be a good alternative if life is too hectic to allow for set counselling sessions or weekly groups. Ataloss.org provides access to live chat with bereavement counsellors from GriefChat via their website. Many bereavement charities also have telephone helplines.

Bereavement counselling.
Talking to a counsellor can provide a safe place to explore emotions and thoughts, and make sense of your loss. Any qualified counsellor should be able to help, or Cruse Bereavement Support.

CBT (Cognitive Behavioural Therapy).
CBT is a talking therapy that can help you manage your problems by changing the way you think and behave. The NHS website has more information (nhs.uk).

Doctor's referrals.
Doctors generally assist with the more physical symptoms of grief such as insomnia, headaches and chronic fatigue. They can also refer you to a psychiatrist if needed, to help with post-traumatic stress disorder or clinical depression. However, you may find that it is quicker to access emotional support through bereavement charities as mentioned above.

It's not unusual to feel that no one really understands our loss, perhaps especially if it was out of the ordinary. Maybe our partner has died at a young age, or we have lost a child, or our loved one has died through suicide or murder, for example. Look for websites, support groups or befriending for your particular circumstances, as finding others who 'get it' without the need for explanation can really help. The search facility on ataloss.org can help you find the right specific support. Having friends, counsellors or fellow mourners who truly care and understand can be an important anchor.

REMEMBER

- Taking time to look after yourself is vitally important.
- It *is* OK not to be OK – it is not a sign of weakness to reach out for help.
- You may find that you need different types of support throughout your bereavement journey.

CHAPTER FOUR

UNDERSTANDING THE JOURNEY

'Moving on, as a concept, is for stupid people, because any sensible person knows grief is a long-term project. I refuse to rush. The pain that is thrust upon us let no man slow or speed or fix.'[5]

– Max Porter

Grief can feel like a never-ending valley. We may start to ask ourselves, 'How long will I feel like this?' but unfortunately, there is no prescribed timeline for grief – it is not a linear process. Each person will experience it differently and you may find that it follows a general path but often circles around in unpredictable ways, and takes a lot longer than you (or others) might

[5] Max Porter, *Grief Is The Thing With Feathers* (Faber & Faber, 2015) p.99.

initially expect. There are various ways of describing the experience of grief, called 'models', which some people find helpful as ways to understand what they are going through. However they are by no means universal to every person's experience, so don't worry if they don't resonate with you. We will look at four of them here.

MODEL 1: GROWING AROUND GRIEF

When we are first bereaved, we can feel that it will be utterly impossible to ever move on from our grief. It is what we think about morning, noon and night and our loss affects every part of us. Dr Lois Tonkin, a grief counsellor, suggests that rather than thinking about 'moving on' from our grief, we can instead grow around it. This can be illustrated by imagining grief as a ball and life as a container.

In the immediate days and weeks after loss, the ball of grief is so big that life seems completely taken up with grief. In time however, rather than grief shrinking, the container expands. This is when we find ourselves more able to face challenges and find capacity for other things in life, such as managing household tasks or meeting up with friends. As this process continues, the ball stays its original size but the container expands further as we return to work, take up new hobbies or develop new relationships. Grief remains, but it no longer fills our life; rather, we have grown around our grief.

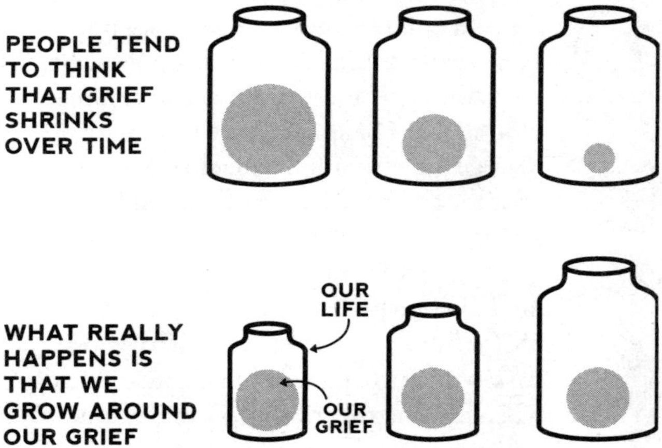

> 'During a support day for bereaved parents I learned to see grieving in a different way – not as a path we have to walk through until we leave the pain behind, but as a process where the pain of loss is always present, but our lives expand around it. From the point where grief dominates every thought and emotion, I found that I began to have the capacity to manage other things. I remember how guilty I felt the first time I laughed out loud; it felt wrong somehow, but there was absolutely nothing to feel guilty about. As the years went on, I discovered that there was space in my life for fun and laughter. We still have 'Ben days' – a shorthand we all understand as a day when for whatever reason, we find ourselves remembering our loss and 'what could have been' – but even these days are now bittersweet as it reconnects us with Ben.
>
> Understanding grief in this way answers those two big questions many bereaved parents have: "Will it always hurt like this?" and "Will I forget?". It answers both with a very firm, "No". Our grief will always be part of us and we can pick it up and remember our child as though it was yesterday, but our lives have grown and there is space for other things as well.' – DAVID, AFTER THE DEATH OF HIS SON

MODEL 2: CONTINUING BONDS

Continuing bonds grief theory is another way of thinking that pushes back against the idea of grief being linear – i.e. that it is an event on a timeline and therefore we will feel it less as we get more distant from it.[6] It suggests instead that it is normal to preserve a bond with the person who has died. This means there is no obligation to 'let go' of the deceased, and that it's normal to stay connected to our loved one.

FINDING COMFORT THROUGH MAINTAINING A CONNECTION WITH THE PERSON WHO DIED BY MARKING ANNIVERSARIES, VISITING SPECIAL PLACES OR KEEPING THEIR THINGS CLOSE BY

[6] Dennis Klass, Phyllis R. Silverman, Steven Nickman, *Continuing Bonds: New Understandings of Grief* (Taylor & Francis, 1996).

This will look different for each of us, but we can keep that connection through retaining items of theirs, visiting places that were special to them, or marking anniversaries – anything that helps us in our grief.

MODEL 3: DUAL PROCESS

The dual process model of grief focuses on two different ways of behaving in grief – 'loss-oriented' and 'restoration-oriented' – and explains that these are states that we move in and out of.[7] 'Restoration-oriented' behaviour focuses on the practicalities of life now that our loved one has gone. This might include getting on with household tasks, or even taking on a big work task in order to distract us from our grief for a while. 'Loss-oriented' behaviour focuses on our loss, which means it can bring up a lot of emotions. This might include crying, looking at old photos, reminiscing or visiting a place that was special to our loved one.

Dual process recognises that we will oscillate between facing and avoiding our loss, and both aspects are necessary. We cannot mourn all the time, but we cannot

[7] Margaret Stroebe and Henk Schut, 'The Dual Process Model of Coping with Bereavement: Rationale and Description', *Death Studies*, 23 (3), 1999, pp197–224.

always be 'coping', either. The overall idea is that it is OK to experience grief in doses, moving from one state to another, and that some days will be better than others – often with no recognisable pattern.

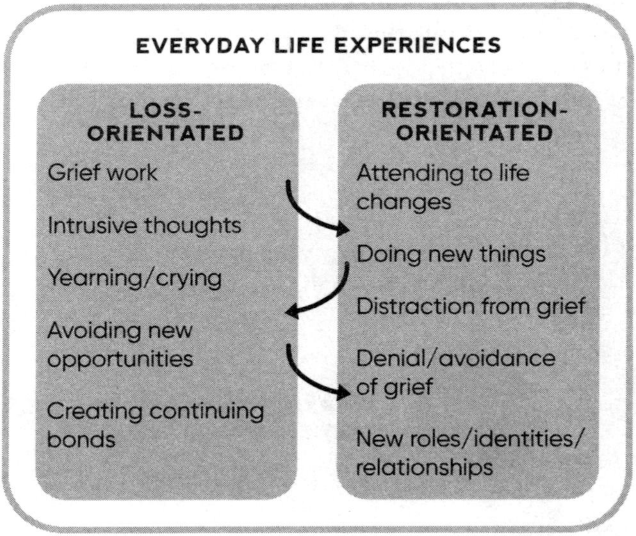

MODEL 4: FOUR TASKS OF MOURNING

This focuses on four tasks that form a part of the grieving process, according to psychology professor William J. Worden. This can help us view grief as a process we can walk through by actively engaging with the tasks (although we may not necessarily do everything in order and some tasks may need to be revisited).

ONE — **ACCEPTING THE REALITY OF THE LOSS**

TWO — **WORKING THROUGH THE PAIN AND EMOTIONS OF GRIEF**

THREE — **ADJUSTING TO A 'NEW NORMAL' WITHOUT OUR LOVED ONE**

FOUR — **FINDING A CONNECTION THAT ENDURES**

The first task is to accept the reality of the loss, and attending the funeral or memorial is often the start of this process. The second is to work through the pain of grief, experiencing and processing a range of different emotions. What is important in this task is acknowledging and understanding these emotions and their effect. The third task is to adjust to an environment where the deceased loved one is missing. This will happen over a period of time, and will look different for everyone. For example, it might involve dealing with waves of sadness, making financial adjustments or living alone. The final task is to find an enduring connection with the deceased as we embark on life without them. This does not mean that everything is 'fixed', but that we are able to continue life with our loved one still in mind.

FIND WHAT WORKS FOR YOU

You may find one of these ways of thinking about grief more helpful than others, or you may find none of them particularly relate to how you are feeling. No one model should be taken as a rule, as often grief does not conform to a recognisable pattern. The point is simply to try to help you visualise your grief and give you language to articulate how you are feeling.

Whether we can relate to one of these models or not, it can be helpful to acknowledge and unpick all the different losses we are facing. If we have lost our partner early in life, we may also be mourning the loss of the opportunity to have children together, for example. A bereaved parent can feel the loss of future hopes and dreams, perhaps the anticipation of having grandchildren. If our parent or someone from an older generation has died, or a sibling, we might mourn the loss of a connection to our childhood and our past. The realisation that we are now the 'older generation' may bring the inevitability of our own deaths to the front of our minds. Feeling lost or unmoored, especially if there are no parental figures left, can be a common feeling. As we begin to understand all the different aspects of our loss, we can find a way to come to terms with them.

'There are many things on the grief journey that trip you up, often unexpectedly. As my sister had children, milestones they reach are double-edged – to be celebrated proudly, but also mourned that my sister is missing each one. Anniversaries and birthdays are obvious ones that are going to be hard. But, as I am now an only child, I hadn't anticipated the heartbreak of wanting to share simple things with my sister, and no longer being able to: the comedic antics of ageing parents, the frustrations of parenting similar-age children, or a memory that no one but me can remember and she is not here to validate. Looking through old photographs and knowing there will never be any fresh ones to share can be devastating.

I will never move on from my sister, but I will move forward. With time and support, painful wounds of grief and loss can heal. Our lives will always bear the scars, but life can become worth living again and our siblings' legacies live on through us.' – GEORGIE

REMEMBER

- There is no prescribed path or timeline for grief.
- Grief models may be helpful to understand what you are going through.
- No one model fits every experience of grief.

CHAPTER FIVE

EMBRACING LIFE AGAIN

'"It is an amputation," said one of the letters I got when Gavin died – a good analogy. Nothing can put back what's gone, but sooner or later the person who has lost a leg learns to walk with a crutch, the woman with only one hand left somehow manages to cope – even if there are phantom pains in the limb that's no longer there.'[8]

– Katharine Whitehorn

Going from the immediate shock of bereavement to the resumption of normal responsibilities can be a rocky journey, and often feels like it has to happen too quickly. Many people who work feel they are not afforded the

[8] Katharine Whitehorn, 'You have to learn in another country, where you're an unwilling refugee', *The Guardian*, 8 November 2005.

time off that they need. Some of us may have children or elderly relatives who still need to be looked after and so we haven't had time and space to completely stop. If finances are tight or work needs attending to, there can be a pressure to return to our jobs quickly. However, while we can't put a stop to all that needs doing, we can ask for some help.

> 'A wise friend told us, "There's enough you have to go through; don't put yourself through stuff you don't have to do." You do have some choices about what you do and don't do. You may have children you need to care for, or other responsibilities, and that's important, but let others help you with other things which don't have to be done by you ... or just choose not to do them.' – JANE

Our loss may have brought new responsibilities our way too. When a next of kin dies, wading through the paperwork associated with bereavement can feel like too much – it can be a good idea to ask a trusted friend to help with it if possible.

If we have lost the person we shared our life with, we might find we have to take on new things, such as managing finances or cooking regularly. It may mean we are now the main earner for the first time and feel the weight of that shift. Or perhaps we have lost a parent or mentor figure and it feels like a major anchor for our life – someone we looked to for practical support and guidance – has gone. If there is a surviving parent who is now more dependent on us emotionally or practically, that can cause added strain.

If people are offering to help, do take them up on it whenever possible, and do think creatively about ways to give yourself space. Could someone at work take over extra responsibilities to cover your workload for a little while? Or is there someone you can ask to babysit for a few hours?

> 'I was able to build up a network of those who supported us with cooking, housework, the kids' homework or by being positive male role models, for example. I thought carefully about who I asked to do what, as different people are good at different things. I learned that I wasn't imposing. People want to help, to do something, as they are grieving too. I also asked people who had memories of Tony and connections with him to talk to the kids about him, to help keep their memories of him alive.'
>
> – RUTH

Not allowing ourselves the time to grieve will take its toll, whether immediately or further down the line. Our stress triggers are very sensitive directly after bereavement, which means we may overreact to minor pressures. The answer to this is not to suppress our emotions, as that will negatively impact our physical and mental health, but to take time to address them. It is good both for us and those around us when we take time to grieve. It is important to let others help and not try to do everything ourselves (and to ask for help if we need to).

FACING LONELINESS

Those of us who are retired or cannot work for any reason may be overwhelmed by feelings of loneliness and isolation. For those who live alone it can be particularly hard, especially if this is a new situation as a result of our loss. Those who go out to work may find arriving home to an empty house excruciatingly difficult, as the reality of life as it now is hits hard at that moment each day.

> 'When two people have shared a life together, it's not just the loss of the individual but also the loss of the pattern of their shared life, the daily rituals, sometimes their social circle.' [9]
>
> – ANDY LANGFORD, DIRECTOR OF CRUSE BEREAVEMENT CARE

Having someone to talk to can really help stem the tide of loneliness, so do try to reach out to those you trust if you can. Arranging with a friend to call them every few days or once a week for a chat may help. Once you feel up to it, joining a local group or volunteering can help you establish new social links and help you feel less alone. Even something as simple as having a friend stay over for a movie night can help stem the feelings of loneliness, as can finding online forums, perhaps centred around an area of interest to you.

GOING BACK TO WORK

Returning to work or education after whatever bereavement leave has been granted will be a different experience for each one of us. If you're in work, your employer may offer generous bereavement leave, only a little or have no formal policy at all. For parents who have lost a child, Jack's Law, introduced in early 2020,

[9] Harriet Sherwood, 'Prince Philip: Experts tell of trauma caused by death of a lifelong partner', *The Guardian*, 11 April 2021.

allows bereaved parents two weeks off work but only for children under eighteen, and two weeks is nowhere near enough for most people.

Some employers only accept that an employee needs longer than a few days of bereavement leave if they are signed off work by a doctor, while others allow for a reasonable length of time plus a slow transition back. Negotiating bereavement leave can be an added stress at a time when we feel incapable of dealing with it. When letting colleagues know of our loss it is worth preparing for a wide range of reactions from them, some of which will be helpful and some not (see Chapter 6 for more on this).

Each one of us will have our own individual way of dealing with our grief and how we would prefer others to deal with it too. Some of us will want people to acknowledge our loss openly, while others of us will feel too sensitive for such conversations in the early days of returning to work. Whatever your preference, be aware that it can be emotionally draining to have the same conversations over and over again with colleagues. It can be helpful to have one conversation with your line manager before you return to work, so that they can relay how you would like people to react to your return. Alternatively, you may like to meet your colleagues socially before returning. This can help you set the tone for how you would like them to respond to your loss.

It can feel quite overwhelming to return to work at first, so ask if there is an option to stagger the return. Focusing may be difficult for a while, so it may be helpful to write everything down and also ask a trusted colleague to check your work over to begin with. Having a quiet space, such as your car, to escape to for a break can be helpful, and you may want to consider having snacks, tissues and a pillow on hand there. Alternatively, ask a trusted close colleague to be there for you to talk to in your most vulnerable moments, or to go for a walk with you during lunch breaks regularly. Be aware that there may be times (such as anniversaries) when you need extra support further down the line.

It is common when we have experienced loss to feel that work suddenly seems trivial. We can find work processes tiresome and get impatient. Bearing this in mind, be patient with yourself and try not to make any decisions in haste. It may be tempting to hand in your notice, but take time to reflect carefully before you make that kind of decision.

HELPING CHILDREN RETURN TO SCHOOL

As well as negotiating their own feelings about returning to work, some parents will also be preparing their children to go back to school. If our partner has died and the children have lost their parent, or someone else very close to the whole family, we face the challenge of helping our children to return to their routines too. We can want time to stand still, and keep our children with us for as long as possible, but going back to their usual everyday activities can help them. There can be added complications if schools are not as accommodating or understanding as they could be, so it can help to have someone else you trust helping you as you seek the support you feel your children need. If you have lost a child, taking the other children to school can be very distressing as you see your child's friends and their parents. Let friends go with you or take your children for you if possible, until you are able to go on your own.

Schools and universities may give bereavement leave and take the grieving process into account by allowing extra time in exams (or may even postpone them). However, not all do this and so some students may have to return before they feel they are ready. Do try to ensure you have good support systems in place with friends and family who can be confided in if this happens.

FINDING A 'NEW NORMAL'

Coming to terms with the fact that the old normal is not coming back can be extremely painful and hit us afresh again and again – sometimes when we are least expecting it. Learning to live in the light of what has happened can feel like a loss in itself.

However difficult it feels at first, it can be helpful to identify things to look forward to. That could be pizza night on Friday, a weekly phone call with a friend, a daily short walk in nature, a weekend away in a month or a holiday next year. Go gently, but do intentionally put things in the diary that you usually enjoy and allow yourself to do so – even if it feels difficult to begin with. It can be painful if relationships change in the wake of bereavement. If we have lost a partner, for example, sometimes old friendships can fade away, as socialising with 'couple friends' may feel awkward. This can be hard to deal with on top of our grief. However, developing new interests, hobbies and cultivating new friendships will be possible in time.

REMEMBER

- Pace yourself where possible.
- Be honest about your needs if/when returning to work, university or school.
- Identify things that you might enjoy, put them in the diary and try to enjoy them.

CHAPTER SIX

COPING WITH OTHERS' RESPONSES

'"You must put it to one side now and look to the future ..." You must keep your mouth shut and stop telling other people to do impossible things. How would you feel if I told you that you "must win the women's bobsleighing race in the Winter Olympics?"'[10]

– **Virginia Ironside**

Although it can seem so unfair when we are already grieving, at times we will probably have to deal with those around us saying unhelpful or insensitive things too. It is therefore helpful to be prepared that even those we love may upset us – albeit most likely unintentionally.

[10] Virginia Ironside, '*You'll Get Over It*': *The Rage of Bereavement* (Penguin, 1997), p.119.

The fact is, most people, especially those that love us, want to help but they just don't know how to. Feeling completely ill at ease but desperate to show us they care, they may offer platitudes and empty phrases that they hope will help. The trouble is that in the midst of grief, such things can sound hollow and clichéd. Some phrases will obviously sound trite and irritating, such as someone saying, 'He's with God now' when the person was a lifelong atheist. But there are many other comments that can be extremely hurtful to us.

> 'When my mum died, lots of people would say they were sorry and then ask how old she was. I knew it was irrational, but I felt really hurt, as if they thought it wasn't that bad a loss because she was in her eighties. Inside I was thinking, "But that's not the point! She was my mum, and now she's gone!"' – LISA

AVOIDING THE SUBJECT – AND EVEN YOU

Many people feel uncomfortable when first talking to someone who has been bereaved, simply because they don't know what to say and don't want to cause any upset. It may mean that some people you expected to be there for you actually avoid seeing you. Those that do engage may avoid the subject completely and, when you mention the person who has died, change the subject. This can seem so hurtful, especially if you are longing to talk about your loved one. Remember, they might be doing it kindly, assuming that talking about them will upset you. If you would like to talk, you may need to let them know.

Often, hearing us speak of the person who has died gives others permission to do so and helps to set a pattern for the future. Unfortunately, some people will clamp down on any mention of the deceased, creating awkward silences. Such silence may fall in a face-to-face conversation, or it may be that friends who used to text and call all the time stop doing so. In such instances, it is quite usual to wish that they would say something, even something ridiculous, rather than nothing at all, as it seems their lack of response is invalidating our grief.

MINIMISING OUR LOSS

We might feel that those around us just don't realise the enormity of our loss. Perhaps it's your friend who has died – but they could have been closer to you than a family member. Maybe your parent was 'a good age', but that doesn't mean their death isn't still devastating.

Sometimes those who lose a brother or sister can feel like 'forgotten mourners', as often everyone focuses on the person's bereaved parents, children or partner. This can leave the bereaved sibling feeling that their grief is being ignored or that their grief isn't valid. This is the relationship that should be the longest in our life – longer than that with a parent or spouse. Even if we fought endlessly with them as children or have had very different lives as adults, the blow can be devastating and feel like we've almost lost a part of ourselves.

Miscarriage and stillbirth, the former of which is not covered by Jack's Law, can feel like ignored griefs too. Mums and dads can feel left to grieve in silence, or can minimise their grief themselves in relation to those who have lost children later in life. If your child died as a newborn, or you had to terminate a pregnancy for medical reasons, you may also feel that your grief is overlooked. Remember that it's OK to grieve these losses, even if others' comments make you feel invalidated. Funerals for miscarriages can be as cathartic as funerals for stillbirths, but it may be too hard for some family members to attend.

PATRONISING RESPONSES

Sometimes people who don't know what to say will put on a look of sympathy and pity that can feel condescending and quite irritating. Unfortunately, although they generally mean well, it may serve to make you feel more awkward. They may also avoid your eyes, adopt a concerned tone in every interaction or be excessively nice. While they are trying to be kind, it can result in making you feel belittled and misunderstood. If someone you see regularly does this, it may be best to have a conversation to let them know how you feel.

Others may see you crying and immediately say, 'Oh, don't cry' because they don't like seeing you upset. They are probably trying to comfort you, but it can result in feeling unhelpful pressure to 'hold it together'. If you have the capacity to do so, you might want to share with your friend that you'll feel better if they let you have a good cry.

It can seem as if some people around us assume that grief is like a bad bout of flu and can be 'got over' in a matter of weeks, months or even days. It can feel patronising to be told to 'get over it' or be asked, 'Isn't it time to let them go?'

> 'I felt that about a year after Bryan's death, my work colleagues were thinking: "OK, you've done that – now move on." I was initially very angry, but then realised that this was mainly due to a lack of understanding. So I stood my ground and told them, "You're not going to get the old Pat back!" I knew that I could never be the same person again. It's OK to do that.'
>
> – PAT

OVERLY EMOTIONAL RESPONSES

Sometimes when people first encounter a bereaved person they gush with emotion about the person who has died, or talk about how upset they are themselves. This can be really difficult to deal with as, at times, they can seem more emotional than we are, particularly if we are feeling numb and unable to cry (this is often the case at funerals). Being faced with someone else who is overly emotional may trigger our grief, or could cause feelings of guilt that we aren't as upset as they are. We could even feel like we have to offer comfort to them, which can be draining and cause us to feel a bit resentful.

BE HONEST – WITH YOURSELF AND OTHERS

While it may not feel fair that those around us keep responding to us in ways that are irritating and unsupportive, we can try to assume the best of them – that they don't realise what they are doing. But you may also want to take note of who you are finding it helpful to be with during this time, and whose company is less helpful. It is often surprising which friends drift away and which remain; which are draining and which are supportive. It's OK to choose who to spend your time with. You might feel the need to take a step back from those who are upsetting you and lean into those who you feel are being most supportive at this sensitive time – and it is absolutely fine to do that.

You may feel you want to challenge those with the most irritating responses, to let them know how unhelpful they are being. Try to be realistic though as to whether you really have the energy for that sort of conversation while you are grieving. Preparing ahead of time for some of the worst clichés can help you to navigate them more easily, although be aware that how you respond to each encounter will depend on your level of energy and tolerance that day, your degree of relationship to the person and how much their words have hurt you.

It can be really helpful, both for you and the person who is unsure about what to say, if you are very open and honest in your communication with them. You could say, for example: 'When you refuse to talk with me about him, I feel upset, because I need to be able to talk about him with people I trust.'

REMEMBER

- People will say unhelpful and insensitive things – but it will usually be unintentional.
- Don't feel guilty if you need to take a step back from those who you are finding difficult for a time.
- You might want to work out beforehand how you want to respond to any particularly unhelpful phrases that people use.

CHAPTER SEVEN

MANAGING FAMILY RELATIONSHIPS

'For a few minutes, Ethan was almost submerged in the sadness of having to talk about his own mother's funeral, but the next moment, he had jumped out of that puddle and was focusing on the prospect of a day off and playing with his cousins! Not for the first time, I wished I could be him, just for a day, just to be able to escape the deluge of adult questions about the future. I too wanted to be able to jump out of that puddle and think about simpler things.'[11]

– Simon Thomas

We all grieve differently, and this is true within our families too. Each person will have their own way of dealing with their grief, so it can be helpful if we try to

[11] Simon Thomas, *Love, Interrupted* (Trigger, 2019) p.176.

be gentle and supportive with one another, particularly when emotions are heightened. Some may withdraw or busy themselves with tasks, while others may need to talk things through many times in order to process and find support.

When our emotions are heightened, and we are struggling with our own grief, it can be hard to see someone dealing with theirs in such a different way, and this can cause strain within the family. There may be issues of guilt or blame too – 'Why didn't I/you call him back that evening?' or, 'Why didn't you look after them better?'. Anger can become an especially intense emotion in our grief, depending on the circumstances of death.

> 'I don't like being helpless, but I was unable to do anything to make it better. The day became a blur as the paramedics arrived. We were taken to the police station, identified Ben's body and began the awful process of telling friends and family. When your child is born, no one gives you a job description, but surely keeping your child alive would be first on the list? On that basis I felt I had failed, both as a father and as a husband. I had been unable to protect my son from falling and unable to protect my family

from pain. I was overwhelmed not only with my own grief but also with feelings of guilt and helplessness. I tried to 'be strong', but my strength just disappeared in the whirlwind of emotions.

We returned home and each member of our family dealt with their emotions in their own way. My wife talked and talked over endless cups of tea and cake. My eight-year-old daughter bounced in and out of grief as though she were jumping in puddles, while my eldest son, just entering his teenage years, simply withdrew into himself and wouldn't be reached. I responded by keeping myself busy, first with the funeral and practical details and later with a myriad of projects. I must have given the impression of managing my emotions well because a few weeks after the funeral, one of the ladies at church pulled me aside and asked, "I can see that you're OK, but how is Jane?" Inside I wanted to scream: "I'm not OK, my world has fallen apart and I don't think I'll ever be OK again".'

– DAVE, ON THE ACCIDENTAL DEATH OF HIS 11-YEAR-OLD SON

How we respond to others during bereavement may not be reflective of how we respond in calmer moments. Emotions are closer to the surface, and we may find ourselves lashing out unexpectedly – even at the smallest of things. Others who are grieving may lash out towards us or others too.

We may feel our close family members are not giving us what we need in our grief, and they may well feel the same about us. We may not understand what's going on for them – and vice versa. Remember that each individual is on their own journey, and needs to find the pace that is right for them. Try to be considerate of one another.

If you feel a particular responsibility to support those around you who are also grieving, try not to suppress your own feelings. For example, perhaps your brother or sister has died, and you feel a sense of obligation to look after your distraught parents. Such a scenario can lead to the phenomenon of 'delayed grief', where a person pushes aside their feelings immediately after the death. Months or years later, the devastating reality of the loss hits and can be overwhelming.

CONFLICT AND TENSION IN FAMILY RELATIONSHIPS

Bereavement can, of course, also expose and magnify tensions that were already in existence before the person's death.

Conflicts over physical things (such as the will or the deceased's possessions) or arrangements over the funeral can be among the hardest to deal with. These are things we can often fixate on to try and minimise the pain of loss. We may have sentimental reasons for wanting to own an object that our loved one was fond of, but it may be meaningful to other family members too and navigating this can feel like a minefield at times.

> 'I can still remember the day that we sorted through Mum's clothes and jewellery. Being the only one who was a similar size to her before she got ill, it was an easy process for me to be able to choose items I wanted to take and wear to remember her. But when it came to her jewellery, my sister, daughter and nieces all wanted to choose something too. I remember telling myself that they all needed something too, but it was hard when someone else chose an item I would have liked. I kept telling myself I had other things, and we could all remember her – and smile when we saw one another wearing a piece of her jewellery. It has taken time, but that is exactly what has happened.'
>
> – CLAIRE

It might be that one member of the family is keen to empty the house or clear away the loved one's possessions straight away, as they find it painful to see those reminders of their loss all around them. Another may feel they are being rushed, and are just not ready to take that step yet. As far as possible, try to nurture good relationships with other family members, considering carefully the decisions that will affect you all. Especially if you are feeling emotionally raw, try to take a step back from any heated conversations and remain respectful even if you don't feel it.

When tense moments do occur, it is best for everyone to try to pause and get some perspective. We can all remember that grief looks different for everyone and those who are not used to showing emotion may only show anger, which is actually masking feelings of vulnerability. It may even be necessary to get some physical distance, and wait until everyone has calmed down to speak again. Sometimes, rifts may open that can only be healed years into the future, as each person needs time to work through and process their emotions. Reconciliation may be a long process.

Handling 'silent tension' can be especially difficult. If there are issues that stem from events before or after a loved one's death, it can be hard to deal with a person who is full of simmering anger. It may be necessary to get a neutral mediator involved, for example if the funeral is still in the planning stages. Giving space for a calm discussion about each person's respective feelings can help build empathy for one another, which may open up the opportunity to grieve together rather than staying angry.

It may be that long after the death, there are still fractured relationships between family members. You may decide you want to take some steps to repair a relationship or want to let go of bitterness and anger against that person for the sake of your own mental health. Grief counselling can be very helpful for this, as can symbolic acts of forgiveness. There is an opportunity for this at the end of *The Bereavement Journey* programme (thebereavementjourney.org).

HELPING CHILDREN GRIEVE

While we are dealing with our own grief, those of us with children – whether parents or other caregivers – have the added responsibility of sharing the news of the loss and then helping them walk through their own grief.

It can be hard to know how to break the news of a death to a child or children of different ages. We may realise it's best to be specific if they are teenagers, but this is true even with young children. While we may be tempted to use expressions such as 'Granny's gone to sleep' or 'Mum's gone to heaven', children are very literal and this can lead to them being afraid to go to sleep, or asking why Mum can't come back from heaven. It's important to use the words death, died and dead with children, although it feels somehow kinder not to – and can be hard to say to begin with. Be very precise about minor details that children ask about. Some children worry that dead people feel pain or might move, or have other concerns that would not occur to an adult.

Children are likely to have questions about what happens after death, and so it can be helpful to consider how to answer those questions beforehand, or how to help them explore for themselves what they might believe. If you feel that you don't know, be honest with them about that. You could share that some people believe different things about life after death. Be OK with not having all the answers – children don't need us to be able to fix their grief; they simply need us to be there for them in it.

Reading books designed to help children with bereavement (see Useful Resources on page 113 for some suggestions) or finding creative ways to express grief can be helpful. Younger children might like to draw pictures of the person. Creating a memory box or scrapbook together as a family may be helpful for all of you. Older children and teenagers may find writing in a journal or composing letters to the person who has died very cathartic. Be aware that children may seem to grieve less than us. A young child may find it easier to accept the passing of an aunt, uncle or grandparent due to it being a more distant relationship. But in cases of a closer relative or friend's death, it can be that they are grieving differently, not less.

Children may oscillate between feeling very sad and being able to function normally when grieving – more so than adults. Young children may cry and feel overwhelmed with sadness – so much so that you are at a loss to know how to help them – and then a few moments later be happily playing. This happens because they cannot cope with sad feelings for long, and need something to distract them. However, it does not mean that they are not grieving. Older children and teenagers may sink themselves into their hobbies, schoolwork or a hectic social life to avoid feeling the pain of grief. They may need reassurance that it is OK to talk about it, but may choose to talk to friends rather than parents.

> 'A few friends got exactly what I needed. They sat with me, sometimes talking, often not. We played games on the PlayStation or darts in my room. They listened when I needed to talk and didn't offer platitudes. They allowed me to get ridiculously angry at tiny things and seemed to understand where that anger came from.'
>
> – JON, WHO WAS 14 WHEN HIS BROTHER DIED

If your spouse or partner has died and you are now caring for children alone, the thought of doing so without their help may seem just too hard. Having to share the news of their mother or father's death will feel excruciating, and dealing with the endless questions children have may be exhausting. Try not to brush those questions aside, and don't stop talking about your partner – the shared memories will build bridges between you in your grief and help each of you.

TV presenter Simon Thomas, in his book *Love, Interrupted,* shares very honestly about his wife dying suddenly and how both he and his eight-year-old son dealt with it. They became 'Team Thomas' and Simon talks about how often his son would help him carry on when he felt it had all become too much. At times, he would ask, 'What would Mummy have said?', which often helped them in difficult situations and kept her memory alive.

Children with learning difficulties or other disabilities may find bereavement especially difficult. Some will need more frequent reminding than other children that death is permanent, and they may not understand abstract concepts like an afterlife. Grieving may also look very different for them; they may process more internally than externally. Concrete activities may particularly help them, such as listening to audio or video recordings from the person who has died or looking at photographs.

As your child's caregiver, it will be important to adapt how you talk about death to your child's age and level of understanding as they grow and learn.

REMEMBER

- Each member in a family will grieve differently.
- If tensions and conflict arise, it may be best to give one another space.
- Children can be very matter-of-fact about death, and jump from feeling sad one moment to playing the next.

CHAPTER EIGHT

FAITH IN THE MIDST OF GRIEF

'We were even told "Blessed are they that mourn" and I accepted it. I've got nothing I hadn't bargained for. Of course, it is different when the thing happens to oneself.' [12]

– C.S. Lewis

Grief can shake our beliefs and assumptions about the world to the core. We know that we each experience bereavement differently, and we all have to filter it through the lens with which we view the world. Anglican minister Yvonne Tulloch has run workshops on questions of faith with bereaved people for many years. She notes that some of the most common

[12] C.S. Lewis, *A Grief Observed: Readers' Edition* (Faber & Faber, 1961, 2015), p.30.

questions at this time, from people with a religious faith or not, are about God – questions such as: 'Why did God let this happen?' 'Where is God?' 'I thought God was supposed to be good?' It can also be a time of questioning our own mortality and what happens after we die. 'Is there a heaven?' 'Will I see them again?' 'Can I get in touch with them?'[13]

All of these questions are normal, although not everyone will ask all of them. As we have said before, loss affects each of us in different ways, and this is no exception.

DON'T DENY THE QUESTIONS

Questioning is a normal part of coming to terms with a death. For those who are familiar with the Psalms of the Bible, it can be comforting to know that they are full of questions: raw, honest outpourings of emotion. This can seem quite foreign to those who are used to a British 'stiff upper lip' method of dealing with grief, but many find it refreshing to discover a place where they can see their own emotions mirrored, which can help them voice their own out loud. For example, Psalm 22 starts off with the raw emotion of feeling abandoned:

> My God, my God, why have you forsaken me?
> Why are you so far from saving me, so far
> from my cries of anguish?

[13] Yvonne Richmond Tulloch, *Faith Questions in Bereavement* (thebereavementjourney.org)

> O my God, I cry out by day, but you do not answer, and by night, but I find no rest.
>
> – PSALM 22:1-2

Having a faith does not mean that we have to shut down the gut-wrenching agony of our 'why?'s' and 'how could you?'s' addressed to God. Being open and honest about how we feel, with all our doubts and questions, is all part of processing our grief. But, again for those familiar with the Bible, there is the promise that God understands our pain, and not only that, he is with us in it. As Lewis B. Smedes says: 'God's own answer to suffering is to join it, to feel it, hurt with it. A sufferer screams to God in the all-wrongness of his life, "Why have you abandoned me?" God answers by joining him in life's most horrible wrongness.'[14]

When we are already navigating grief, it can feel totally disorientating to have our usual worldview crumbling under its weight. We might find, in the midst of pain, that we voice sentiments and questions about our faith that would never normally come out of our mouths. Some Christians may also experience a lack of God's presence, right in the moment when they feel they desperately need him, which can be bewildering and add to the questioning. Yvonne Tulloch experienced

[14] Lewis B. Smedes, *How Can It Be All Right When Everything Is All Wrong?* (Harold Shaw Publishers, 1999, first edition Harper & Row, 1982) p.105.

this after her husband died and says, 'Whatever our faith background, we are likely to question our beliefs, whether consciously or unconsciously, and possibly lose, for those of us who had it, our sense of God's presence … When there's a storm, dark clouds gather overhead, and we cannot see the sun. But the sun is there, whether we sense it or not, and in time, the clouds begin to disperse and rays of light break through.'[15]

Others of us might find we cling tighter to our faith than ever before, but not give ourselves space to question – squashing down any doubts that may try to surface in our minds. Or, maybe for the first time, we look for something outside of ourselves to help us make sense of all that has gone on. Remember, whatever your background, it is natural to have questions. Feeling bereft, angry, confused or overwhelmed is normal.

LOOKING FOR ANSWERS

Sometimes other people can feel threatened by the tough, unanswerable questions we raise. They may try to 'comfort' us with the idea that there is some grand plan behind our suffering. The human tendency to wish away pain can result in people around us refusing to engage with the deep questions that grief provokes. It may be that others keep insisting that everything happens for a reason. Christian author Kate Bowler discovered this when she was diagnosed with Stage 4 cancer:

[15] Yvonne Richmond Tulloch, *Faith Questions in Bereavement*, p.4-5

> 'People want me to reassure them that my cancer is all part of a plan. A few letters even suggested it was God's plan that I get cancer so I could help people by writing about it. People are certain it is a test of my character or proof of something terrible I've done. They want me to know without a doubt that there is a hidden logic to this seeming chaos. They tell my husband, while I'm still in the hospital, that everything happens for a reason, and then stammer awkwardly when he says, 'I'd love to hear it. I'd love to hear the reason my wife is dying.'[16]

When we are grieving it can be easy to shut ourselves off from others. But it is important to realise that there will be people who will want to walk alongside us in this most difficult of times. Often the best support will be from those who are honest enough to say when they find a question unanswerable – people who are there to experience our confusion and doubts with us.

Sometimes churches or other places of worship can handle grief badly, but most want to help, however clumsily they may express it. Many faith communities help those who have been bereaved by providing meals,

---

[16] Kate Bowler, *'"Everything happens for a reason" and other lies I've loved'*, *Ted.com*, 2018.

helping to clean and babysit or offering other services. This can be an easier way to receive support than lots of well-meaning questions. Others may run support groups or courses, such as *The Bereavement Journey* (thebereavementjourney.org), which helps navigate and process the most common aspects of grief, and allows space for asking questions. If your local faith community offers to help, let them know what kind of things would be best for you.

Another natural part of bereavement is to think that we have seen the person who has died:

> 'My dad died very unexpectedly and it was the first bereavement I'd experienced. I vividly remember walking down the road one afternoon and noticed a car just like my dad's, parked a bit further down the road. Not only was it the same car, it looked like my dad was in the driving seat, but it drove off before I got the opportunity to take a proper look. For one moment I thought perhaps he hadn't died after all. It was only when I mentioned it to someone else that I found out this is quite a common occurrence.' – PAULA

As well as seeing someone, we may feel a sense of their presence with us, or smell the aroma of their perfume or aftershave. Some will find great comfort in this, while for others it can be distressing or scary. Grief is not just an emotional response – our brain's processing and thinking can be impacted and may take some time to register the fact that a person has gone. Sensing the person, even talking out loud to them, is a way of staying connected, although both may diminish over time.

Sometimes the desire for connection is so strong that we actively seek out ways to contact the person, through mediums or spiritualists for example. Most major religions warn against this, and whilst such contact can sometimes seem to bring some comfort, it can also lead to increased grief and negative emotions. Similarly, using AI and digital avatars of the one we've lost may bring solace, but can prevent us from coming to terms with the reality of our loss, thus prolonging our grief. Talking through how we feel and maintaining connection through some of the positive ways mentioned earlier in this book are much better for our spiritual and emotional health.

OTHER PEOPLE'S BELIEFS

Our friends or other members of our family might have different beliefs to us, and they may be quite vehement in expressing these even when we and/or they are in the throes of grief. The extreme emotions of bereavement tend to blunt or remove the usual social filters, and this can be difficult to deal with. It is worth taking a step back from any disagreements that might arise to remember that you are both grieving. Being compassionate towards one another will be more helpful than continuing the argument (see Chapter 7 for more on dealing with conflict).

UNRESOLVED IS OK

The questions we can have in the wake of bereavement may be resolved quickly, or they may linger for years. Some of us might take a long time to re-evaluate our faith in the light of our experiences. It's likely, though, that our faith will show the marks of our bereavement and be forever changed. That could involve either an estrangement from God, or a deepening relationship with God. If you find you are wrestling with deep questions, you may wish to seek guidance from someone at your local place of worship, or read Yvonne Tulloch's *Faith Questions in Bereavement*, which addresses ten common questions.

Ultimately, we may have to accept that there is no answer to some of our questions. When we ask 'why', often what we need is not so much an answer, as for people (and God) to be with us in our pain. One of the major aspects of the Christian faith is hope, even when our questions are unresolved. Psalm 147 verse 3 tells us that 'God heals the brokenhearted and binds up their wounds'.

REMEMBER

- Grief can cause us to question our worldview.
- It's OK to have questions – but do realise there may not be answers.
- Try not to cut yourself off from your community or family, but take things at a pace that is right for you.

CHAPTER NINE

REMEMBERING YOUR LOVED ONE

'What is grief if not love persevering?'[17]

– Vision, from the Disney+ series WandaVision

When we first lose someone we love, thinking about them may seem very painful. We long to still have them with us, and it's hard to accept that's no longer possible. Finding ways to include the memory of them in our lives can help us come to terms with our loss.

Grief counsellors recommend that instead of trying to move past our grief, we should recognise that our world has changed irrevocably. In this new world, we continue our relationship with the person we have lost in different

[17] *WandaVision*, 'Previously On', dir. Matt Shakman, 2021.

ways. So we may decide to continue to celebrate their birthday, keep their bedroom intact or tend their grave regularly. It can also help to continue to talk about the person who has died with other people who loved them.

WAYS TO REMEMBER

There are so many different ways we can choose to remember our loved ones. Many people find that having objects to touch, smell or look at helpful, and despite some thinking it is unhealthy, this is actually a very natural way to grieve. Having some things that still smell like our loved one can be comforting, so we may wish to keep an article of clothing that smells like the person we've lost. The sense of smell is directly connected to memory in the brain[18], so smells especially can be of great comfort. Similarly, an object that our loved one often touched can have great meaning. Buying your wife's perfume and spraying it on your own or your children's pillows, or cooking a meal that the child you lost used to love, could help. A bereaved younger sibling may find great comfort in hand-me-downs such as clothing and toys.

Some people find it helpful having lots of photos of the person they have lost around the house. Others prefer not to see the images daily but instead have photos in albums or online. If the person who has

[18] Colleen Walsh, 'What the nose knows', *The Harvard Gazette*, 27 February 2020.

died lived with us, we may or may not wish to clear away their belongings. Some prefer to keep a deceased person's space intact, but equally, others may want to clear the room and simply keep a few items as a way of remembering them. Do what's right for you and don't feel you have to rush to get rid of everything.

Talking about our loved one in everyday conversation (when it is less painful to do so) can also help. Sharing funny or poignant stories about them with people who also knew them can be a great comfort. This can continue to be helpful as we remember our loved ones at times such as Christmas or their birthday.

'I was dreading the first Christmas after Mum died, but actually it was comforting being with family and enjoying the usual celebrations, and we had a good day together. The first Mother's Day was harder. I bought a bunch of her favourite flowers for the house, and remembered her with gratitude when I saw them.' – LISA

DEALING WITH ALL THINGS ONLINE

It isn't just a person's physical belongings that will need sorting through after they have died. If your loved one was active online, they will have left what is known as a 'digital afterlife'. Emails, computer files, cloud storage, social media accounts and online password accounts are all part of this. Details of how they wanted all this managed may have been listed in their will, including who they wanted to have access, but it may be that nothing was said. Many social media accounts are operated under a licence that is not transferable on death. Therefore, if no one has access to the person's passwords, access will not be granted. Any digital assets (including photographs, which may have sentimental value, and even assets with monetary value, such as Bitcoin) would lie dormant and eventually become part of the unclaimed assets register. Some of the technology giants such as Google, Apple and Facebook have addressed this by giving users the opportunity to stipulate what happens to their accounts ahead of time.

As long as access has been provided to the deceased person's passwords, there may well be digital photographs and other memories to be distributed among family in order to remember the loved one. It is also possible to memorialise, delete or leave open their social media accounts, depending on their wishes or, if none were specified, the decision of the family.

It may be that the decision has been made to use social media to put out a death announcement. Do remember that this may well garner a lot of sympathetic comments that could be hard to read, so it may help to ask someone less directly affected by the loss to put out the announcement and handle the comments. Alternatively, manage people's expectations by saying that you appreciate all comments but will not be responding individually.

DEALING WITH HURDLES AND 'TRIPWIRES'

We may be very aware of the hurdles we will face after losing a loved one – such as the first time we go out without them, or family events, birthdays and Christmas. We can anticipate those and take time to think about how we might want to include our loved ones in such moments. We can also be kind to ourselves if we know we will find something too difficult and communicate to others that we have decided not to do it.

> 'Tell people how you are feeling – what you are finding difficult and what would be helpful. I remember times when I was so hurt about the way people behaved and when they said or did the 'wrong' things. But over time I realised that if I haven't told them how I feel and what

I need, they can't be expected to automatically know. So be honest with people.

You don't have to go to something or do something if it is just going to be too hard. Be kind to yourself. If you are only able to go to part of a wedding, stand at the back of a school event (and cry!) or can't go to a family event which will just be too tough – that is OK.

Different family members experience these hurdles differently. Talk to each other, including siblings, and find out what works for you. Remember, pretending a hurdle isn't there will inevitably result in a stumble; you're much more likely to jump it if you look it in the eye!' – CATHERINE

There are other times when we 'trip' over things that we couldn't have foreseen – something that triggers our grief unexpectedly. This may happen through any of our senses; perhaps their favourite food is being cooked by someone else, we realise while walking round the supermarket that we don't have to buy certain products any more, or we hear their favourite song on the radio.

> 'I was doing the dishes at the sink and started to wash a marmalade jar that was now empty. At the same moment I realised with a jolt that this was the last jar of the marmalade that Evelyn had made, and tears filled my eyes. Over many years she had made her own marmalade, which we both enjoyed at breakfast. Now there will be no more.'[19] – TONY HORSFALL

We can't predict these moments, so can't prepare in advance – but we can be kind to ourselves when they happen. Rather than getting angry and upset with ourselves, we can sit in the moment, acknowledging what has happened and perhaps telling someone. In time, we will find we can deal with such tripwires without being floored by them.

There will be certain dates when we might feel our loss acutely – such as our loved one's birthday, Mother's or Father's Day, or the anniversary of their death. Turning off social media on such days can be helpful, as it may trigger grief. It may be that you need to take some time for yourself on these anniversaries – and it is absolutely OK to say so to those around you.

---

[19] Tony Horsfall, *Grief Notes* (BRF, 2022), p.25.

> 'It's hard to think how to better cope with tripwires, other than to recognise that they are going to happen and are painful. Be kind to yourself. I remember thinking after one such tripwire, 'Why was that so hard?' and beating myself up about the way that I reacted, but being honest with myself and allowing myself to feel the pain was far more helpful.' – NIGEL

Recalling fond memories (either with family or alone) can help with milestone moments, so you might like to hold on to some photographs or other items that will remind you of happy times. Despite the sadness this may cause at first, in time you will appreciate being able to look back on them.

These forms of grieving can help you come to terms with your loss. The road of grief may never entirely end, but it is possible to leave the acute pain of loss behind without letting go of your loved one. They will always be a part of your story.

'Our son Ethan died when he was two and a half, and it left us with a hole in our family that felt like a gaping, open wound. His new baby brother was very young, and we were struggling. Mark and I knew that we wanted our baby and any subsequent children to grow up being aware that Ethan was a part of our family and feeling like they had always known their big brother. We have had two more children who never met Ethan, but I like to think that through the way we have sewn Ethan's memory into the fabric of our lives, they know him.

We decided to plant a tree in a nature reserve in memory of Ethan. We felt uncomfortable taking our young family to a graveyard and thought a tree was a more fitting place to walk and remember their brother. As the children and the tree have grown together, we have made things to hang on Ethan's tree, taken photos each year in front of it and it has provided us with a special focal point, full of life.' – RACHEL

LEARNING TO LAMENT

Psychologist Dr Kate Middleton talks of the importance of 'learning to lament'[20], which simply means 'giving yourself the time and space to express and process difficult emotions'.[21] Most of the emotions that we experience during grief are hard to describe, and so lament can often be best expressed in creative ways, such as painting or keeping a journal. Other simple ways to lament include singing, reading through a loved one's favourite book or exchanging memories of that person with others. It may take other forms, such as a pilgrimage – whether secular or religious. New Zealander Julie Zarifeh walked the famous Camino de Santiago to help her work through the experience of losing both her husband and son in a short space of time.[22] Whatever form of lament we may choose to engage with, it provides an outlet for the intense emotions of grief, providing space for messy, unpackaged sorrow, even if it sometimes seems that our society would prefer we suppress it.

YOU DON'T HAVE TO 'MOVE ON'

People may tell us that we need to 'move on' after a bereavement, or that in time we will 'get over' our loss. In reality, 'moving on' can be an unhelpful way to think

[20,21] Kate Middleton, '*Learn to Lament*', Mind and Soul Foundation, 20 May 2020.

[22] Emma Clifton 'How walking the 800km Camino de Santiago helped me work through my devastating grief', *Now to Love*, 25 August 2019.

about it. Grief doesn't necessarily get smaller; instead, our lives adjust around the grief. (See page 40 for more on this.)

Psychologist William J. Worden talks about 'emotionally relocating' the person who has died.[23] This means adjusting from a relationship with someone who is alive to a continuing relationship with someone who is not physically there. This is not about forgetting the person who has died but coming to terms with a 'new normal'. We can continue the bond with the deceased person by remembering them and incorporating them into everyday conversation.

If we experience someone telling us to move on, if we have the energy for it, we can respond with something like: 'I'm focusing on just getting through each day at the moment' or 'I need to feel these emotions, not repress them.'

We can try to be gracious in our responses, as people who say these things usually only want to spare us pain (see Chapter 6 for more on this). But the encouragement to do so by bulldozing through our emotions is rarely helpful. In her TED talk, author Nora McInerny talks about the emotions that the phrase 'moving on' raised in her after her husband's death:

> 'By any measure, life is really, really good, but I haven't 'moved on'. I haven't moved on, and I hate

---

[23] Details in his book *Grief Counseling and Grief Therapy: A Handbook for the Mental Health Practitioner.*

that phrase so much, and I understand why other people do. Because what it says is that Aaron's life and death and love are just moments that I can leave behind me – and that I probably should ... I've not moved on from Aaron, I've moved forward with him.'[24]

REMEMBER

- It can be helpful to keep some of the person's belongings and to find ways to include them in your life moving forward.
- You can learn how to negotiate hurdles and tripwires.
- To move forward you don't have to leave the person behind.

[24] Nora McInerny, 'We don't "move on" from grief. We move forward with it', *Ted.com*, 2018.

CHAPTER TEN

HOW OTHERS CAN HELP

'I see people, as they approach me, trying to make up their minds whether they'll "say something about it" or not. I hate if they do, and if they don't.'[25]

– C.S. Lewis

Though some people's ill-chosen words and actions can cut us deeply when we are grieving, the kindness of sensitive friends and relatives can also help in our healing. We will differ in what we find most helpful from other people. Some of us will prefer that others ask as little as possible about our grief, and keep the conversation on neutral topics. Many of us will

[25] C.S. Lewis, *A Grief Observed: Readers' Edition* (Faber & Faber, 1961, 2015), p.8.

want those around us to acknowledge our loss, even if they aren't sure what to say. For others, in-depth conversations about our feelings with close friends and family will help us to process our grief. Our preferences will depend on many things, including personality, whether we are introverted or extroverted and our cultural background and upbringing too.

Our emotions will probably be all over the place during our grief, and this will affect how we respond to other people's attempts at comfort. Author Virginia Ironside notes that we might find someone's words 'heart-warming on a Tuesday, and mindless nonsense on a Wednesday'.[26] Despite this, we can still communicate to our friends, relatives and employers what we find helpful and not (see Chapter 6 for more on unhelpful responses). This chapter aims to equip you with the tools to do that.

'I DON'T KNOW WHAT TO SAY'

The culture in much of the Western world actively avoids talking about death, which can make it very hard for others to offer meaningful support. As we discussed in Chapter 6, platitudes, avoidance and condescending sympathy are common. We genuinely do not have a shared cultural language for talking about grief, so other people may falter in their attempts to be helpful. It is a

[26] Virginia Ironside, '*You'll Get Over It*': *The Rage of Bereavement* (Penguin, 1997), p.ix.

normal human response to try to 'fix' the pain we see in others who are hurting, so this may be a reaction we experience a lot.

Some people will also be scared of upsetting those who are grieving, whether out of genuine concern or uncomfortableness with naked emotion. This can mean that they refrain from talking about the person who has died. This may come across as ignoring our loss, which can be very painful. If we feel able to, we could raise the issue with them and let them know if we do want to speak about the person we've lost. For some people, this can be the green light to share in our grief that they have been waiting for.

For those of us who do not show our emotion on the surface, or if we are feeling numb, our friends and family may struggle to understand. Everyone's way of grieving is different, and it can be hard if we feel pressured to demonstrate how upset we are in front of others who expect us to react in a certain way.

Friends and family may say, 'Let me know what you need!' but this can be hard to do, especially if we aren't sure ourselves. We may hesitate to take them up on their offer for fear that they didn't really mean it, or we don't want to bother them. The people who step in with a specific offer of help can often be far more helpful. Visiting on a Thursday afternoon, bringing round a casserole, walking the dog – these concrete actions are usually far more useful than a vague promise of assistance. It is easier to respond to specific offers, and these gestures can really help us when thinking about what we need feels like just another pressure. The willingness of friends and family to take the initiative is precious.

> 'A couple of months after my brother died, my friend Caron repurposed a chocolate box, decorating it and calling it Sabina's Sunshine. She invited my friends to write notes about what they appreciated about our friendship and put them in the box. I have my box of sunshine next to me at my office desk. When I'm feeling particularly sad, or before a challenging meeting, I open the box and read a note. After my mother died, I asked my friends for objects they could contribute to a comfort box that kept one of my five senses occupied: essential oils, chocolate, beautiful pictures, fabrics with different textures, chimes, and so on.' [27] – SABINA NAWAZ

[27] Sabina Nawaz, 'Returning to Work When You're Grieving', *Harvard Business Review*, 28th April 2017.

If others offer to help, we can try to let them know what practical things they could help with – perhaps those things we are struggling to get around to or are finding difficult. Many people will be relieved to feel that they are able to help in any capacity. One woman collected WhatsApp voicemails for a friend in which mutual friends voiced their love and support for the person grieving. Others may offer to babysit or tend to the garden. Each one of us will differ in what we find helpful, but, even if you don't think you need something, do consider taking up the offers made to you as you may find they help more than you think they will.

WORKPLACE SUPPORT

Workplaces will vary greatly in how much support they offer to a bereaved employee, partly because the law around bereavement is open to the employer's interpretation. Unfortunately, we may find that there is not much understanding or acknowledgement of our loss.

Employers who handle bereavement well, however, may find themselves with a very grateful (and consequently loyal) employee. If an employer offers paid time off for bereavement, use as much as you need without feeling guilty. If your paid time off comes to an end and you are not ready to go back to work, have a conversation with your line manager to ask whether they would allow for a phased return or for extra breaks in a working day. Many workplaces, especially in education, buy into emotional support packages that offer counselling for employees, so do check whether this is available.[28]

Workplace behaviour is usually oriented towards doing. Grief is different, and cannot be solved by a task-based mentality. It requires making space for the messy and unsolvable during a task-oriented workday. If you have a supportive manager or colleagues, try to help them to support you by communicating what would be helpful. That might be the use of a quiet space when you need a few moments to regroup or an adjustment of deadlines.

> 'I had two days off, the Thursday and Friday, and then the weekend. I was in shock. I was embarrassed. I was hurt that no one from work seemed to care. The week prior, a colleague had been involved in a car accident. She was fine, just a little shaken. She had four days off work and the office sent her a card and flowers. I didn't even get a phone call and when I returned to the office, no one asked how I was.'[28] – REBECCA, AFTER HAVING EXPERIENCED A MISCARRIAGE

[28] Amelia Hill, '"You never stop grieving": why bereaved parents need more than two weeks off work', *The Guardian*, 3 February 2020.

THE IMPACT OF EMPATHY

Author and speaker Brené Brown talks about empathy and why it has such a great impact: 'Empathy is feeling with people ... Rarely can a response make something better. What makes something better is connection.'[29] Sometimes, surprisingly, the best support comes from people who may not have been bereaved themselves (or whose bereavement experience may look very different), but who are willing to take the time to get on our emotional level and connect with us. 'Empathy is not connecting to an experience, it's connecting to the emotions that underpin an experience.'[30]

In bereavement, loneliness can occur when people don't try to connect because they don't want to get it wrong or hurt us further. But the people who do try – even if they stumble along the way – can become our biggest help in the midst of bereavement. Consider asking them to spread the word to others that doing something is better than doing nothing, and that even a simple gesture such as a heartfelt message or a freezer meal will be much appreciated.

---

[29] Brené Brown on Empathy', *YouTube*, 10 December 2013.
[30] Brené Brown, *Dare to Lead* (Penguin Random House, 2018), p.140.

> 'While I don't expect most people to remember exact dates of things, one of my good friends has my significant dates (the loss of our baby and the loss of my sister) on her Google calendar to recur annually. Just knowing that she does that so she can check in on me around tricky anniversaries really helps.' – GEORGIE

REMEMBER

- Often people don't reach out because they don't know what to say – not because they are being intentionally hurtful.
- You can let people know what practical help you would find most useful.
- Ask if there is an emotional support package available at your workplace.

NEXT STEPS

'When I say, "Oh, Aaron is ..." it's because Aaron still is. And it's not in the way that he was before, which was much better .... It's just that he's indelible, and so he is present for me.'[31]

– Nora McInerny

Reinvesting in life in the wake of bereavement can be a slow and at times arduous process. As we have established, grief is not something we get over, but a complete change from one state of life to another. After the initial shock, we can be left wondering how we will operate in this new way of being. It can be quite

[31] Nora McInerny, 'We don't "move on" from grief. We move forward with it', *Ted.com*, 2018.

overwhelming to consider the uncharted territory of life after our loss.

Right now you might be wondering if the pain will ever get less, or asking why you still feel a certain way. You may long for someone to give you a schedule for when you can expect to feel 'better'. Though each person grieves differently, many find that, over time, the sharp and intense pain of grief diminishes. The struggle to think beyond the short term becomes more manageable and it is possible to find things to look forward to. To start with, these may be very small steps – this is completely normal. You may find yourself oscillating between optimism for the future and waves of grief, but remember to go at your own pace.

There is no hurry and it is better to take things a day at a time, reaching out for help when things feel overwhelming, rather than trying to rush the process.

> 'It may seem impossible when we are in the midst of grief to think that we could ever be happy again, but we will be. Slowly, with the passing of time and the brave work that grieving well requires of us, we will emerge into the brightness of a new day. Joy will return.'[32]
>
> – TONY HORSFALL

[32] Tony Horsfall, *Grief Notes* (BRF, 2022), p.14.

USEFUL RESOURCES

NATIONAL SIGNPOSTING SERVICE

AtaLoss provides the UK's bereavement signposting service. Their website offers information and signposting to national, specialist and local bereavement services, including telephone helplines. Visit ataloss.org for comprehensive, up-to-date details of resources, information and organisations that can support you, many of which are free to access.

The following details and telephone numbers may be helpful if you do not currently have internet access, or feel unable to search online.

WHEN YOU NEED TO TALK

- Samaritans: phone 116 123 at any time, 24 hours a day.
- Cruse National Bereavement helpline:
  0808 808 1677.
- National Bereavement Service:
  0800 0246 121.
- SHOUT:
  Text: 85258
  giveusashout.org

PRACTICAL GUIDANCE

- Step-by-step guide to what to do after someone dies, including registering the death, arranging the funeral, help with funeral costs, dealing with the estate, and information on your benefits, pension and taxes. gov.uk/when-someone-dies
- Practical advice for the recently bereaved (including a PDF checklist): Search ataloss.org for 'recently bereaved'.
- Applying for probate: gov.uk/applying-for-probate
- Bereavement Service Helpline, for help and advice on bereavement benefits you may be entitled to, including a Funeral Expenses Payment claim. 0800 731 0469.
- What does a funeral director do for you? Search nafd.org.uk for 'The role of a funeral director'.

GENERAL BEREAVEMENT SUPPORT

- *The Bereavement Journey* consists of six sessions that use films and small group discussions to help guide you through your grief. Groups are run across the country and online. (thebereavementjourney.org)
- Cruse Bereavement Support (cruse.org.uk) have a telephone helpline (0808 808 1677), online chat service and local branches that provide group sessions and one-to-one support.

- Search the NHS website (nhs.uk) for 'Grief after bereavement and loss' or 'CBT'.
- British Association for Counselling & Psychotherapy (bacp.co.uk) has a directory of therapists.
- Counselling Directory (counselling-directory.org.uk) has a national directory of counsellors.

SPECIALIST BEREAVEMENT SERVICES

Specific age or gender support

- StrongMen (StrongMen.org.uk) offers peer-to-peer support and dedicated retreats for men who have been bereaved.
- Child Bereavement UK (childbereavementuk.org) helps children who are grieving and supports parents in talking to their children about bereavement. They offer a helpline, live chat via their website or email. 0800 02 888 40.
- Grief Encounter (griefencounter.org.uk) also helps children and young people who are bereaved, through a helpline, live chat or email. 0808 802 0111.
- Age UK (ageuk.org.uk) provides general support for older people through their helpline, including the bereaved and lonely. 0800 678 1602.

Baby loss

- Saying Goodbye (sayinggoodbye.org) provides comprehensive information, advice, support, counselling and therapy to anyone who has suffered the loss of a baby, at any stage of pregnancy, at birth or in infancy. 0300 323 1350.
- Tommy's (tommys.org) provides support to anyone who has lost a baby through miscarriage, stillbirth, neonatal death or termination for medical reasons.
- Petals (petalscharity.org) offers support from a dedicated counsellor for those who have lost a baby.
- The Miscarriage Association (miscarriageassociation.org) offers information, online support groups and a support helpline: 01924 200799.
- The Lullaby Trust (lullabytrust.org) supports anyone affected by the death of a baby or young child. Their bereavement support helpline is available on 0808 802 6868.
- Sands (sands.org.uk) offers support to anyone affected by the death of a baby. Their telephone helpline is free to call: 0808 164 3332.

Loss of a partner/spouse

- Care for the Family (cff.org.uk) provides support events and befriending for those widowed young (up to the age of 50, or older with dependent children). 029 2081 0800.
- WAY (widowedandyoung.org.uk) provides peer-to-peer support to anyone who has lost a spouse or partner before their 51st birthday. 0300 201 0051.
- Way Up (way-up.co.uk) is an active online self-help group aimed at providing mutual support to those who have been widowed primarily (but not exclusively) in their 50s and 60s.

Bereaved parents and siblings

- Care for the Family (cff.org.uk) provides support events and befriending for bereaved parents, and support events for bereaved siblings, both online and in person, as well as the Brothers & Sisters Life after Loss private Facebook group for those who have lost siblings to share with one another. 029 2081 0800.
- Surviving the Loss of your World (slowgroup.co.uk) offers supports for bereaved families (parents and siblings). 07532 423 674.
- The Compassionate Friends (tcf.org.uk) provides support for bereaved parents and bereaved siblings. 0345 123 2304.

Suicide and sudden death

- Survivors of Bereavement by Suicide (uksobs.org) has several options on their website, or you can call their helpline: 0300 111 5065.
- Sudden (sudden.org) supports those who have lost a loved one suddenly. Helpline: 0800 2600 400.
- The Lucie Blackman Trust (lbt.global) offers support to families whose loved one has died abroad.

Murder/manslaughter

- The Compassionate Friends (tcf.org.uk) has specific information for families affected by murder. 0345 123 2304.
- The National Homicide Service offers support to families bereaved by murder/manslaughter. 0300 303 1984.
- Support after Murder and Manslaughter (samm.org.uk) supports those bereaved through murder or manslaughter. Helpline: 0121 472 2912.
- Government guidance on deaths abroad due to murder or manslaughter can be found on gov.uk – search 'Death abroad through murder or manslaughter' and 'Coping with death abroad'.

EMPLOYMENT-RELATED RESOURCES

- Sabina Nawaz's articles on Harvard Business Review 'How to Offer Support to a Grieving Colleague' and 'Returning to Work When You're Grieving' are helpful reads: search the article titles on hbr.org
- For information on the law and your rights regarding bereavement leave and pay, acas.org.uk has useful advice and a helpline you can call: 0300 123 1100.

FAITH RESOURCES

- Association of Christians in Counselling (acc-uk.org) has a directory of Christian Counsellors in the UK.
- Jewish Bereavement Counselling Services (jbcs.org.uk) offers bereavement support to Jews who are grieving: call 020 8951 3881.
- Muslim Youth Helpline (myh.org.uk) offers bereavement support to young Muslims who are grieving: 0808 808 2008.
- Children of Jannah (ChildrenofJannah.com) provides grief support and information for bereaved Muslim parents and families.
- Sikh Helpline (sikhhelpline.com) is a general helpline for Sikhs but also offers bereavement support: 0845 644 0704 or 07999 004 363.

- For humanists, humanistgrief.com offers general advice and resources.
- You may also find it helpful to talk directly to your local faith leader.

FURTHER READING

BOOKS

Books marked with an asterisk * are written by authors coming from a Christian faith perspective.

General bereavement

Yvonne Richmond Tulloch, *Faith Questions in Bereavement*. A compassionate look at the big questions about life and faith that can arise after loss. Available from thebereavementjourney.org *

Wendy Bray, *The Path Not Chosen: Beginning the Journey of Loss and Bereavement*. A booklet describing the grieving process to help people through their grief journey.*

Wendy Bray and Diana Priest, *Insight Into Bereavement*. Discusses grief through the lens of the Christian faith.*

Carla Fine, *No Time to Say Goodbye: Surviving The Suicide Of A Loved One*. The author draws on her own experiences as well as those of others to explore the complex feelings of grief that arise in the wake of a loved one's suicide.

Virginia Ironside, *'You'll Get Over It': The Rage of Bereavement*. The author writes directly and honestly about her own and others' experiences of grief, addressing the often-neglected anger that many people feel during bereavement.

Elisabeth Kübler-Ross, *On Grief and Grieving: Finding the Meaning of Grief Through the Five Stages of Loss*. A guide to grief by a psychiatrist, which developed the now-famous theory of the stages of grief: denial and isolation, anger, bargaining, depression and acceptance.

Pablo Martinez and Ali Hull, *Tracing the Rainbow: Working Through Loss and Bereavement*. The authors look at bereavement both through firsthand experiences and through the lens of a psychiatrist, exploring what grief is and what others can do to help.*

Claire Musters, *Every Day Insight: Disappointment and Loss*. A 30-day Christian devotional the author wrote by her mother's bedside in the final days of her life.*

Penelope Swinthinbank, *Scent of Water*. A devotional for the first six months after bereavement that includes entries for 'special days' such as the funeral, Christmas, birthdays and anniversaries.*

Multiple bereavements

Malcolm Duncan, *Good Grief*. The author shares his personal experiences of grief and insight with a Christian ethos.*

Nora McInerny, *It's Okay to Laugh (Crying Is Cool Too): A Memoir*. The author talks about losing her husband, father, and second baby in the span of six weeks through a series of personal essays.

Jerry Sittser, *A Grace Disguised: How the Soul Grows through Loss*. The author shares from his own tragic loss of losing his mother, his wife and his young daughter in a car crash and reveals his belief that, despite the pain, new life is possible – one marked by spiritual depth, joy, compassion and a deeper appreciation of simple and ordinary gifts.*

Loss of a spouse

Joan Didion, *The Year of Magical Thinking*. The author writes about the loss of her husband and her daughter's illness, and her attempts to make sense of the year that followed.

Tony Horsfall, *Grief Notes: Walking through loss*. Based on the diary entries the author wrote in the first year after his wife's death.*

C.S. Lewis, *A Grief Observed*. Charts his raw, honest reflections on the death of his wife Joy from cancer. It includes his meditations on how a Christian reconciles their faith with the reality of death and the awfulness of grief.*

Max Porter, *Grief is the Thing with Feathers*. A poetic novella exploring the author's feelings on the death of his wife and raising their sons without her through the metaphorical crow, which symbolises grief.

Simon Thomas, *Love, Interrupted: Navigating Grief One Day at a Time*. Television presenter Simon Thomas talks about the sudden death of his wife Gemma and his own journey through grief and becoming a single parent to their son.*

Loss of a child

Zoe Clark-Coates, *The Baby Loss Guide: Practical and compassionate support with a day-by-day resource to navigate the path of grief*. A personal guide to baby loss from the author's experience of losing five babies, including a practical and compassionate day-by-day resource for the first sixty days.

Philippa Skinner, *See You Soon*. A personal account by the author of losing her son to a heroin overdose in his early twenties and how she grieved in the face of the stigma surrounding substance abuse deaths.*

Nicholas Wolterstorff, *Lament for a Son*. A personal account by the author of losing his son at the age of twenty-five in a mountain climbing accident.*

Loss of a sibling

Julie Bentley and Simon Anthony Blake, *Sisters and Brothers: Stories about the death of a sibling*. A collection of twelve short stories, all from the perspective of someone who has lost a sibling in adulthood.

TJ Wray, *Surviving The Death Of A Sibling: Living Through Grief When an Adult Brother or Sister Dies*. Based on the author's experience of losing her 43-year-old brother, this book aims to reassure adults who have lost a sibling that they are not alone in their struggle.

Alan D Wolfelt, *Healing the Adult Sibling's Grieving Heart: 100 practical ideas after your brother or sister dies*. A concise and actionable guide to help anyone who has lost a sibling as they work through their grief.

Facing suffering (including bereavement)

Kate Bowler, *Everything Happens for a Reason and Other Lies I've Loved*. A Christian author diagnosed with stage four cancer articulates the grief of facing her own mortality and the hollowness of the platitudes others offer her to try and explain suffering.*

Pete Greig, *God on Mute: Engaging the Silence of Unanswered Prayer*. The author shares his own experience of the miraculous power of prayer alongside the pain of unanswered prayer and considers the common human struggle to find faith within that paradox.*

Paul Kalanithi, *When Breath Becomes Air*. A book by a neurosurgeon who was diagnosed with inoperable lung cancer and died during the writing of this book. It explores how to live well in the face of death.

Lewis B. Smedes, *How Can it Be All Right When Everything is All Wrong?* The author is a former professor of theology and explores how we don't have to deny difficulties to be open to God.*

HELPING CHILDREN UNDERSTAND BEREAVEMENT

Randy Alcorn, *Tell Me About Heaven*. A story book about a boy coming to terms with the loss of his grandma.*

Jenny Album, *Tell Me about Heaven, Grandpa Rabbit!* An illustrated storybook for 4-6 year olds to help them come to terms with losing someone special.*

Pete English, *Tough Stuff – Someone has died* (ataloss.org). A journal for late primary to early secondary age children, to work through with their parent, carer or on their own.

Patrice Karst, *The Invisible String*. Helps children to understand that they are loved, whether their parents are near or far. Not only about loss and grief, but includes that.*

Mike Peacock, *The Party in Heaven*. The author presents a story about heaven aimed at comforting bereaved children. Dyslexia-friendly font.*

Jayde Perkin, *Mum's Jumper*. An illustrated book to help children understand grief through the metaphor of growing into a jumper.

Michael Rosen, *Sad Book*. Illustrated by Quentin Blake and written about the death of Michael Rosen's son Eddie, this picture book explores feelings of grief and sadness in an accessible way.

Doris Stickney, *Waterbugs and Dragonflies: Explaining Death to Young Children*. Explains the concept of death to children through a story about a colony of water bugs in a pond.

ABOUT CARE FOR THE FAMILY

Established in 1988, Care for the Family is a charity based in the UK, but with an increasing reach internationally. Our aim is to support families whatever their circumstances. We provide this support, online and in person, for parents, couples and those who are bereaved, through events, courses, podcasts, volunteer befrienders, books and other evidence-based, accessible resources. We also train those who work with families whether in a professional or informal capacity.

Stay in touch

For the latest news, event and training information, helpful articles and resources follow us online or get in touch.

029 2081 0800
cff.org.uk